## LIVING AND D

After studying more than 20,0[0] [who] had near-death experiences, Dr. Küb[ler-Ross finds] that they report remarkably similar experiences—regardless of the subjects' age, religious background, or nationality. This essay details what we can expect at death, notably that "the dying experience is almost identical to the one at birth. It is a birth into a different existence."

## THERE IS NO DEATH

Drawing on her own life and her work with the dying, Kübler-Ross makes a convincing case for the assertion that "nothing in life need be negative—even death." She notes that those who have had near-death experiences no longer fear dying—indeed, some recall reluctance to return from "the other side."

## LIFE, DEATH, AND LIFE AFTER DEATH

This essay addresses life's most difficult questions, expressed here by a nine-year-old cancer patient as "What is life, what is death, and why do young children have to die?" The amazing research and data on life after death reported here provide more than answers—they offer hope for all of us.

## DEATH OF A PARENT

A sensitive yet practical discussion of one of the most difficult times anyone must face. Using case studies from her practice, Dr. Kübler-Ross begins with advice for those helping young children deal with a parent's death, then goes on to provide coping strategies for adolescents and adults.

# ON LIFE AFTER DEATH

# ON LIFE AFTER DEATH

**Elisabeth Kübler-Ross**

CELESTIALARTS

*Berkeley, California*

Text design by David Charlsen
Cover design by Ken Scott
Typeset by ImageComp

Library of Congress Catalog Card #91-058674

Part of this book consists of three lectures given by Dr. Kübler-Ross:

*Living and Dying:* A public speech in German with the title "Leben und Sterben", given in December, 1982, in Switzerland.

*Death Does Not Exist:* A public lecture with the title "There is no Death", given in 1977 in San Diego and published the same summer in *The Co-Evolution Quarterly.*

*Life, Death, and Life After Death:* A lecture recorded on tape in 1980; the cassette is still available from The Elisabeth Kübler-Ross Center, Head Waters, Virginia 24442.

These three pieces have been published in German, Dutch, Danish, French, Spanish and Italian with the following titles:

UBER DEN TOD UND DAS LEBEN DANACH
Verlag "Die Silberschnur", GmbH (German)

OVER DE DOODEN HET LEVEN DAARNA
Uigeverij—Ambo BV (Dutch)

DODEN OG LIVET EFTER DODEN
Hans Reitzels Forlag A/S (Danish)

UBER DEN TOD UND DAS LEBEN DANACH
Editions du Rocher (French)

LA MUERTE: UN AMANECER
Ediciones Luciérnaga (Spanish)

LA MORTE E LA VITA DOPO LA MORTE
Edizioni Mediterranee (Italian)

First Printing, 1991
Printed in the United States of America
4 5 — 95 94 93

# CONTENTS

# LIVING AND DYING

**M**any people say: "Of course, Doctor Ross has seen too many dying patients. Now she starts getting a bit funny." The opinion which other people have of you is their problem, not yours. This is very important to know. If you have a clear conscience and are doing your work with love, others will spit on you and try to make your life miserable. Then, ten years later, you are honored with eighteen doctorates for the same work. This is the situation in which I find myself.

After sitting at the deathbeds of children and old people for many years, listening intently to what they are conveying to you, you will recognize that they know when death is approaching. Suddenly, someone will bid you farewell when you are not thinking that death will arrive soon. If you do not push this statement aside, but continue to sit and listen, then the dying one will tell you all he wants to share. After the patient dies you will have a good feeling because you may have been the only person who took his words seriously.

We have studied twenty thousand cases of people all over the world who had been declared clinically dead and who later returned to life. Some awoke quite naturally, others through reanimation.

I want to sum up briefly what every human being is going to experience at the moment of death. This experience is the same for everyone regardless of whether you are an Aboriginal of Australia, a Hindu, a Moslem, a Christian, or an unbeliever. In the same way, this experience doesn't depend on age or economic status. Dying is a human process in the same way that being born is a normal and all-human process.

The dying experience is almost identical to the experience at birth. It is a birth into a different existence which can be proven quite simply. For thousands of years you were made to "believe" in the things concerning the beyond. But for me, it is no longer a matter of belief, but rather a matter of knowing. And I am prepared to tell you how you can obtain this knowledge, provided you really want to know. If you are not interested in knowing about it, it doesn't make any difference because once you have died you will know it anyway. And I will sit there and will be full of joy, especially for those who now say: "Poor little Doctor Ross!"

There are three stages to the moment of death. If you can accept the language used in my conversations with dying children, and which I applied, for instance, in the Dougy letter, then you will accept that the death of the human body is identical to what happens when the butterfly emerges from its cocoon. The cocoon can be compared to the human body, but is not identical with your real self for it is only a house to live in for a while. Dying is only moving from one house into a more beautiful one — if I may make a symbolic comparison.

As soon as the cocoon is in an irreparable condition — be it from suicide, murder, heart attack or chronic disease, it doesn't matter how it happened — it will release the butterfly, your soul so to speak. At this second stage, symbolically speaking, after the butterfly leaves its material body, you will experience some important things which you simply ought to know in order not to be afraid of death anymore.

At this second stage you are supplied with psychic energy, while in the first stage you were supplied with physical energy. In the latter, you still needed a functioning brain, an alert consciousness to communicate with your fellow beings. As soon as this brain, or this cocoon, is damaged, you do not have an alert consciousness any more. At the moment when the latter is lacking and when — so to speak — your cocoon is in such a condition that you could neither breathe nor could your pulse or brain waves be measured, your butterfly has already left the cocoon. This does not necessarily mean that you have died already, but rather that the cocoon doesn't function any more. On leaving the cocoon you reach the second stage, that which is supplied by psychic energy. Psychic and physical energies are the only two which man can manipulate.

The greatest gift God granted man is free will. Among living beings, free will is given only to man. As such, man has the choice to use this energy in a positive or negative way. As soon as your soul leaves the body, you will immediately realize that you can perceive everything happening at the place of dying, be it in a hospital room, at the site of an accident or wherever you left your body. You do not register these events with your earthly consciousness, but rather with a new awareness. You register everything with this new awareness, even during the time your body has no blood pressure, no pulse, no breathing, and in some cases even no measurable brain waves. You realize exactly what everyone says, what they think and how they act. You will later be able to tell in minute detail, for example, that three blow torches were used to cut your body out of the crashed car. It has even occurred that people could recall the exact license plate number of the car that ran into them, and the driver who decided to take off. Scientifically, it is not explainable that someone who does not have brain waves could read a license plate number. (From the scientists, humility is demanded!) We have to accept, in humbleness, that there are millions of things which we cannot understand. This is not to say that those things which we cannot understand do not exist, or are not real simply on the grounds that we are not able to understand them.

If I blew a dog whistle you wouldn't hear it, but every dog could hear it, the reason being that the human ear is not made for the reception of such high frequencies. In the same way, an average man is unable to behold a soul which is out of the physical body while, on the contrary, this stepped-out soul can still register earthly vibrations, and can understand everything that happens at the site of an accident.

Many people have an out-of-body experience during surgery, and in fact are watching the surgeons at work. This fact has to be acknowledged by all medical and nursing staffs, and during their work on the patient they should speak only of matters they believe the unconscious one is allowed to hear. It is sad what is said in the presence of unconscious people as they can often hear every word.

You, too, have to know when approaching the bed of your dying mother or father, who may be in a deep coma, that this woman or man can hear everything you say. At those moments it is not too late to say: "Sorry," or "I love you," or whatever else you want to say. For these words, it is never too late to say them, even to the dead ones, because they can still hear you. Even then you can finish "unfinished business" which you might have carried with you for ten or twenty years. In this way you can unburden yourself of your guilt so that you yourself may live more fully.

In this second stage, the "dead" one will realize that he is whole again. People who were blind can see again. People who couldn't hear or speak can hear and speak again. Those of my patients suffering from multiple sclerosis, being able to move only in a wheelchair and having trouble uttering a sentence, tell me full of joy after they return from a near-death experience: "Doctor Ross, I could dance again." And there are thousands in wheelchairs who during this second stage could finally dance again. Of course, after their return, they are back in their ailing body.

You understand now that this out-of-body experience is an enjoyable and blessed happening. The little girls who have lost their hair from cancer treatments tell me after such an event: "I had my nice curls again." Women whose breasts were removed have their breasts again. They are quite simply whole again, just perfect.

Many of my skeptical colleagues say: "Those cases can be considered projections of wishful thinking." Fifty-one percent of all my cases were sudden near-death-experiences. I do not believe that anyone goes to work dreaming, while crossing the street, that he will in the future remain in possession of his feet. However, suddenly, due to an accident, he sees one of his legs on the road separated from his body. In spite of that, he still sees himself in his near-death experience in full possession of two legs.

All of this is naturally no proof for a skeptic. And in order to calm down the skeptics, we did a scientific project with blind people. Our condition was that we would involve only blind people who had not had any light perception for at least the last ten years. Those who had an out-of-body experience and came back can tell you in detail what colors and jewelry you were wearing if you were present. Furthermore, they can tell you the color and pattern of your sweater, or of your tie, and so on. You understand that these statements refer to facts which one cannot invent. You can recheck the facts providing you are not afraid of the answers. However, if you are afraid of them, then you may come to me like some of those skeptics and tell me that those out-of-body experiences are the result of lack of oxygen. Of course, if it were only a matter of lack of oxygen, I would prescribe it for all of my blind patients. Do you understand what I'm trying to say? If someone doesn't like a certain truth, he will come up with a thousand arguments against it. However, again, this is his problem. One shouldn't try to convince other people. When they die, they will know it anyway.

In this second stage you will also notice that nobody will die alone. When you leave the physical body, you are in an existence where there is no time. That simply means that time doesn't exist anymore. In the same way, one can no longer speak of space and distance in the usual sense because those are earthly phenomena. If, for example, a young American dies in Asia and thinks of his mother in Washington, he will bridge the thousands of miles through the power of thought in a split second and will be with her. In this second stage, there are no distances. This phenomenon was experienced by many people when they realized that somebody who lived far away suddenly appeared in front of them. A day later, a telephone call or a telegram reached them telling of the passing of the one seen, who lived hundreds or thousands of miles away. These people are by nature very intuitive, for normally one doesn't notice this kind of visitor.

On this level you realize as well that nobody can die alone because the deceased one is able to visit anyone he likes. There are people awaiting you who died before you, who loved and treasured you a lot. And since time doesn't exist on this level, someone who lost a child when he was twenty years of age could, after his passing at the age of ninety-nine, still meet his child as a child. For those on the other side, one minute could be equal to one hundred years of our earth time.

What the church tells little children about guardian angels is based on fact. There is proof that every human being, from his birth until his death, is guided by a spirit entity. Everyone has such a spirit guide, whether you believe it or not. Whether you are Jewish, Catholic, or a member of any other religion doesn't matter, for such love is unconditional. This is why everyone receives this gift of a spirit guide. They are the ones who my little children call "playmates." They talk to them and they are fully aware of their presence. But about the time they have to go to school, parents tell them: "You are now a big boy. You go to school. One doesn't play such childish games anymore." In this way you forget that you have spirit playmates until you are lying on your deathbed. A dying old lady conveys to me: "Here he is again." Since I do not know what she is referring to, I ask this lady if she could share with me what she has just seen. She tells me: "You must know, when I was a little kid he used to always be around me. But I have totally forgotten that he existed." A day later she dies, full of joy, knowing that someone who loves her dearly is waiting for her.

In general, the people who are waiting for us on the other side are the ones who loved us the most. You always meet those people first. In cases of very small children — two- or three-year-olds for example — whose grandparents and parents as well as all the other known family members are still on earth, it is mainly their personal guardian angel who receives them, or Jesus, or another religious figure. I never encountered a Protestant child who saw the Virgin Mary in his last minutes, yet she was perceived by many Catholic children. It is not a matter of discrimination, you are simply received by those who meant the most to you.

In the second stage, after you have perceived that your body is whole again and you have encountered your loved ones, you will realize that dying is only a transition to a different form of life. The earthly physical forms you leave behind because you have no need for them anymore. But before you step out of your physical body in exchange for those forms which you will keep for eternity, you pass through a phase which is totally imprinted with items of the physical world. It could be that you float through a tunnel, pass through a gate, or cross a bridge. Having been born in Switzerland, I was allowed to cross a pass in the Alps covered with wild flowers. Everyone is met by the Heaven he or she imagined. For me, naturally, I was allowed to experience this transition by crossing a mountain pass of incomparable beauty. Meadows were covered with the colored flowers of the Alps which I could only compare to a Persian carpet.

After you have passed this tunnel, bridge or mountain pass, you are at its end embraced by light. This light is whiter than white. It is extremely bright, and the more you approach this light the more you are embraced by the greatest, indescribable, unconditional love you could ever imagine. There are no words for it.

If someone is having a near-death experience, he is allowed to see this light only for a short moment. After this he must return. But when you die, I mean really die, the connection between the cocoon and the butterfly (which could be compared with the navel cord) will be severed.

After this, it is not possible to return to the earthly body. But you wouldn't want to return to it anyway, for after seeing the light nobody wants to go back. In this light, you will experience for the first time what man could have been. Here there is understanding without judging, and here you experience unconditional love. In this presence, which many people compare with Christ or God, with love or light, you will come to know that all your life on earth was nothing but a school that you had to go through in order to pass certain tests and learn special lessons. As soon as you have finished this school and mastered your lessons, you are allowed to go home, to graduate!

Some people may ask: "Why do such cute little children have to die?" The answer is quite simple. They have learned in a very short period what one has to learn, which could be different things for different people. There is one thing everybody has to learn before he can return from where he came, and that is unconditional love. If you have learned and practiced this, you have mastered the greatest lesson of all.

In this light, in the presence of God, Christ, or whatever you want to name it, you have to look back on your entire life from the first day until the last. With this viewing of your own life you have reached the third stage. On this level you are no longer in the possession of the consciousness from the first stage, or of the awareness from the second. You are now in possession of knowledge. You know in minute detail every thought you had at any time during your life on earth. You will remember every deed, and know every word that you ever spoke. This recapitulation is only a very small part of your knowing because at this moment you know all consequences resulting from your thoughts, and from every one of your words and deeds.

God is unconditional love. During this review of your earthly life you will not blame God for your fate, but you will know that you yourself were your own worst enemy since you are now accusing yourself of having neglected so many opportunities to grow. Now you know that long ago when your house burned down, when your child died, when your husband hurt himself, or when you yourself suffered a heart attack, all fatal blows were merely some of the many possibilities for you to grow: to grow in understanding, to grow in love, to grow in all those things which we still have to learn. "And instead of using those opportunities wisely," you will repent now, "with every blow I became more and more embittered in such a way that my rage and my negativity grew . . ."

We are created for a very simple, beautiful and wonderful life. My greatest wish is that you will start looking at life differently. If you accept your life as something you were created for, then you will no longer question whose lives should be extended and whose should not. No one would ask if someone should be given an overdose in order to shorten his or her life. But dying must never mean having to suffer. Nowadays, medical science is so fantastic that anyone can be kept pain-free. If your dying ones can be kept without pain, dry and nursed with care, and you have the courage to take them all to your homes — I mean all, if possible — then none of them will ask you for an overdose.

Within the last twenty years only one person asked me for an overdose. I didn't understand why, and I sat down and asked him: "Why will you have it?" And he revealed to me: "I don't want to have it. It's my mother. She cannot take my situation any longer. This is why I promised her to ask for an injection." Naturally, we talked to his mother, and we could help her. You must understand that it was not hate which brought her to this desperate point, it was simply too much for her to endure. No dying patient is going to ask for an overdose provided he is cared for with love, and is helped to finish his unfinished business.

In the same way, I want to point out that it is a blessing to have cancer. I do not want to minimize the bad parts that go along with cancer, but I want you to know that there are thousands of things which are worse than cancer. I have patients with amyotrophic lateral sclerosis, one of the many neurological illnesses where you cannot do anything but watch the process of paralysis continue until you cannot move anymore. Finally, you cannot breathe or talk. I do not know if you can imagine what it feels like to be totally paralyzed from your toes to your head. You are unable to write and to speak, you just can't do anything. If you have heard about such people, let me know. We are in the possession of a helpful communication chart (speaking board) which enables the patient to communicate with you.

**M**y wish is that you pass on to many people a little more love. Think about the fact that those people for whom you select the most costly Christmas presents are often those people you fear the most, and for whom your feelings are the most negative ones. I doubt if it is truly necessary for you to give someone a big present — unconditional love would have been more appropriate. There are twenty million children in the world dying of starvation. Adopt one of those children, and start buying smaller presents. Think about the fact that there are many poor people, even in Western Europe. Share your blessings of wealth. Then, when the windstorms blow into your life, think about them as a present for yourself which will not be seen as such at that moment, but perhaps ten or twenty years later. For they will give you strength and teach you things which, otherwise, you would have never learned. If you — symbolically speaking — get thrown into a tumbler (like a stone), it depends fully on yourself if you get crushed or if you come out of it a polished, sparkling diamond.

I want to assure you that it is a blessing to sit at the bedside of a dying patient. Dying doesn't have to be a sad and horrible matter. Instead, you can experience many wonderful and loving things. What you learn from dying patients you can pass on to your children and to your neighbors, and maybe our world would become a paradise again. I believe now is the time to start.

# DEATH DOES NOT EXIST

**T**his morning I'm going to share with you how a two-pound "nothing" found her way, her path in life. I'm going to share with you how you too can be convinced that this life, this time that you are in a physical body, is a very, very short span of your total existence. It's a very important time because you are here for a very special purpose which is yours and yours alone. If you live well, you will never have to worry about dying. You can do that even if you have only one day to live. The question of time is not terribly important; it is a man-made, artificial concept anyway.

To live well means basically to learn to love. I was very touched yesterday when the speaker mentioned, "Faith, love and hope, but the biggest of the three is love." In Switzerland, you are confirmed when you are sixteen, and you are given a saying that is supposed to be a leading word throughout your life. Since I was one of triplets, they had to find one saying for the three of us. They picked love, faith, and hope, and I happened to be love.

I'm going to talk with you about love today, which is life, and death; it is all the same thing.

I mentioned briefly that I was born an "unwanted" child. It wasn't that my parents didn't want a child. They wanted a girl very badly, but a pretty, beautiful, ten-pound girl. They did not expect triplets, and when I came, I was only two pounds and very ugly with no hair, and it was a terrible, terrible disappointment. Fifteen minutes later, the second child came. After twenty minutes more, a six-and-a-half-pound baby arrived, and my parents were very happy. But they would have liked to give two of them back.

I think that nothing in life is a coincidence, not even my birth, because it gave me the feeling all my life that I had to prove that even a two-pound "nothing" was worthy of living. Therefore I worked very hard, like some blind people do who think that they have to work ten times as hard to keep a job.

When I was a teenager, and the war was over, I needed and wanted to do something for this world which was in such a terrible mess. I had promised myself that if the war ever ended, I would walk all the way to Poland and Russia and start first aid stations and help stations along the way. I kept my promise, and this was, I think, when my work on death and dying started.

I personally saw the concentration camps. I personally saw trainloads of baby shoes, trainloads of human hair from the victims of the concentration camps being taken to Germany to make pillows. When you smell the concentration camps with your own nose, when you see the crematoriums when you are very young like I was, when you are really an adolescent in a way, you will never ever be the same again. What you see is the inhumanity of man, and you realize that each one of us is capable of becoming a Nazi monster. That part of you you have to acknowledge. But each one of us also has the ability to become a Mother Teresa. She is one of my saints — a woman in India who picks up dying children, starving, dying people, and believes very strongly that even if they are dying in her arms, that if she has been able to love them for five minutes, that this makes it worthwhile that they have lived. She is a very beautiful human being, if you ever have a chance to see her.

When I came to the United States after having been a country doctor in Switzerland, and a very happy one, I had prepared my life to go to India. I wanted to be a physician in India like Schweitzer was in Africa. But two weeks before I was supposed to leave I was notified that the whole project in India had fallen through. Instead of the jungles of India I ended up in the jungles of New York, married to an American who took me to the one place in the world which was at the bottom of my list of places I ever wanted to live. But even that was no coincidence, because to go to a place that you love is easy. To go to a place where you hate every bit of it, is a test.

I ended up at Manhattan State Hospital, another dreadful place. Not really knowing any psychiatry, being very lonely and miserable and unhappy but not wanting to make my new husband unhappy, I opened up to the patients. I identified myself with their misery and their loneliness and their desperation, and suddenly my patients started to talk, even people who didn't talk for twenty years. They started to verbalize, and share their feelings, and I suddenly knew that I was not alone in my misery. Suddenly I felt only half as miserable working in a state hospital. For two years I did nothing but live and work with these patients. I spent every Hanukkah, Christmas, Passover and Easter with them, just to share their loneliness, not knowing much psychiatry, the theoretical psychiatry that one ought to know. I barely understood their English, but we loved each other. We really cared. After two years, 94 percent of those patients were discharged, self-supporting, into New York City, many of them having their own jobs and being able to function.

What I'm trying to say to you is that knowledge helps, but knowledge *alone* is not going to help anybody. If you do not use your head and your heart and your soul, you are not going to help a single human being. This is what so-called hopeless, chronic schizophrenic patients taught me. In all my work with patients, whether they were chronic schizophrenics, severely retarded children, or dying patients, each one has a purpose. Each one can not only learn from and be helped by you, but they can actually become your teacher. That is true of six-month-old retarded babies who can't speak. This is true of hopeless schizophrenic patients who behave like animals when you see them for the first time. But the best teachers in the world are dying patients.

Dying patients, when you take the time to sit with them, teach you about the stages of dying. They teach you how they go through the denial and the anger, and the "Why me?", and question God and even reject Him for a while. They bargain with Him, and then go through horrible depressions. Yet if they have another human being who cares, they may be able to reach a stage of acceptance. That is not just typical of dying, and really has nothing to do with dying. We only call it the "stages of dying" for lack of a better phrase. If you lose a boyfriend or a girlfriend, if you lose your job or you are forced to move from your home where you have lived for fifty years and have to go to a nursing home, some people if they lose a parakeet, some if they only lose their contact lenses go through the same "stages of dying." This is, I think, the true meaning of suffering.

All the hardships that you face in life, all the trials and tribulations, all the nightmares and all the losses, most people view as a curse, as a punishment by God, as something negative. If you would only realize that nothing that comes to you is negative. I mean nothing. All the trials and tribulations, the greatest losses, things that make you say, "If I had known about this I would never have been able to make it through," are gifts to you. It's like some-body has to temper the iron. It is an opportunity that you are given to grow. This is the sole purpose of existence on this planet earth. You will not grow if you sit in a beautiful flower garden and somebody brings you gorgeous food on a silver platter. But you will grow if you are sick, if you are in pain, if you experience losses, and if you do not put your head in the sand but take the pain and learn to accept it not as a curse, or a punishment, but as a gift to you with a very, very specific purpose.

I will give you a clinical example. There was a young woman in one of my workshops — they are one-week live-in retreats — who did not have to face the death of a child, but she faced several what we call "little deaths." Not very little in her eyes. When she gave birth to her second baby girl, which she was very much looking forward to, she was told in a not very humane way that the child was severely retarded, in fact that the child would never be able to even recognize her as her mother. When she became aware of this her husband walked out on her, and she was suddenly faced with two young, very needy, very depen-dent children, no money, no income and no help.

She went through a terrible denial. She couldn't even use the word "retardation." She then went through fantas-tic anger at God, and cursed him. First he didn't exist at all, and then He was a mean old you-know-what. Then she went through tremendous bargaining — if the child would at least be educable, or recognize her as a mother. Then she found some genuine meaning in having this child, and I'll simply share with you how she finally resolved it. It began to dawn on her that nothing in life is a coincidence. She tried to look at this child and tried to figure out what purpose a little vegetable-like human being has on this earth. She found the solution, and I'm sharing this with you in the form of a poem that she wrote. She's not a poetess, but it's a very moving poem. She identifies herself with her child and talks to her godmother. She called the poem "To My Godmother."

> What is a godmother?
> I know you're very special,
> You waited many months for my arrival.
> You were there and saw me when only minutes
>     old,
> and changed my diapers when I had been there
>     just a few days.
> You had dreams of your first godchild.
> She would be precocious like your sister,
> You'd see her off to school, college, and
>     marriage.
> How would I turn out? A credit to those who
>     have me?
> God had other plans for me. I'm just me.
> No one ever used the word precocious about
>     me.
> Something hasn't hooked up right in my mind:
> I'll be a child of God for all time.
> I'm happy. I love everyone, and they love me.
> There aren't many words I can say.
> But I can communicate and understand affection,
>     warmth, softness and love.
> There are special people in my life.
> Sometimes I sit and smile and sometimes cry, I
>     wonder why?
> I am happy and loved by special friends.
> What more could I ask for?
> Oh sure, I'll never go to college, or marry.
> But don't be sad. God made me very special.
> I cannot hurt. Only love.

And maybe God needs some children who
    simply love.
Do you remember when I was baptized,
You held me, hoping I wouldn't cry and you
    wouldn't drop me?
Neither happened and it was a very happy day.
Is that why you are my godmother?
I know you are soft and warm, give me love,
but there is something very special in your eyes.
I see that look and feel that love from others.
I must be special to have so many mothers.
No, I will never be a success in the eyes of the
    world.
But I promise you something very few people
    can.
Since all I know is love, goodness and
    innocence,
Eternity will be ours to share, my godmother.

This is the same mother who, a few months before, was willing to let this toddler crawl out near the swimming pool while she pretended to go to the kitchen so the child would fall into the swimming pool and drown. I hope that you appreciate the change that took place in this mother.

This is what takes place in all of you if you are willing to always look at anything that happens in your life from both sides of the coin. There is never just one side to it. You may be terminally ill, you may have a lot of pain, and you may not find anyone to talk with. You may feel that it's unfair to take you away in the middle of your life, that you haven't really started to live yet. Look at the other side of the coin.

You are suddenly one of the few fortunate people who can throw away all the "baloney" that you have carried with you. You can go to somebody and say, "I love you," when they can still hear it. They can skip the schmaltzy eulogies afterwards because you know that you are here for a very short time. You can finally do the things that you really want to do. How many of you truly do the kind of work that you really want to do from the bottom of your heart? If you don't, you should go home and change your work. Do you know what I'm saying to you? Nobody should do anything because somebody tells them they ought to. That is like forcing a child to learn a profession that is not its own. If you listen to your inner voice, your inner wisdom — which is far greater than anybody else's as far as you are concerned — you will not go wrong and you will know what to do with your life. And then time is no longer relevant.

After working with dying patients for many years and learning from them what life is all about, what regrets they have at the end of their lives when it seems to be too late, I began to wonder what death is all about.

In my classroom, a certain Mrs. Schwarz gave us our first account of a patient who had an out-of-body experience. This led to a collection of cases from all over the world. We have hundreds of cases, from Australia to California. They all share the same common denominator. They are all fully aware of shedding their physical body, and death, as we understand it in scientific language, does not really exist. Death is simply a shedding of the physical body like the butterfly shedding its cocoon. It is a transition to a higher state of consciousness where you continue to perceive, to understand, to laugh, and to be able to grow. The only thing you lose is something that you don't need anymore, your physical body. It's like putting away your winter coat when spring comes, you know that the coat is shabby and you don't want to wear it anymore. That's virtually what death is all about.

Not one of the patients who has had an out-of-body experience was ever again afraid to die. Not one of them, in all our cases. Many of our patients also said that besides the feeling of peace and equanimity they have, and the knowledge that they can perceive but not be perceived, they also have a sense of wholeness. This means that somebody who was hit by a car and had a leg amputated, sees his amputated leg on the highway. But when he gets out of his physical body, he has both legs. One of our female patients was blinded in a laboratory explosion, and the moment she was out of her physical body she was able to see, was able to describe the whole accident and describe people who dashed into the laboratory. When she was brought back to life she was totally blind again. This may help you to understand why many, many of these patients resent attempts to artificially bring them back when they are in a far more beautiful, more perfect place.

The most impressive part, perhaps, for me, has to do with my recent work with dying children. Almost all of my patients are children now. I take them home to die. I prepare the families and siblings in order to have "my children" die at home. The biggest fear of children is to be alone, to be lonely, to not be with someone. At the moment of this transition, you are never, ever alone. You are never alone now, but you don't know it. But at the time of transition, your guides, your guardian angels, people whom you have loved and who have passed on before you, will be there to help you. We have verified this beyond a shadow of a doubt, and I say this as a scientist. There will always be someone to help you with this transition. Most of the time it is a mother or father, a grandparent, or a child if you have lost a child. Sometimes it is people you didn't know were "on the other side" already.

We had one case of a child, a twelve-year-old, who did not want to share with her mother what a beautiful experience it was when she died. No mother likes to hear that her child found a place nicer than home, and that's very understandable. But this child had such a unique experience that she needed desperately to share it with somebody, so one day she confided in her father. She told him that it was such a beautiful experience when she died that she did not want to come back. What made it very special, besides the whole atmosphere and the fantastic love and light that most of them convey, was that her brother was there with her, and held her with great tenderness, love and compassion. After sharing this she said to her father, "The only problem is that I don't have a brother." Her father started to cry, and confessed that she did indeed have a brother who died three months before she was born. They had never told her.

Do you understand why I am bringing up examples like this? Many people say, well, you know, they were not dead, and at the moment of their dying they naturally think of their loved ones, so they naturally visualize them. But nobody could visualize a brother they never knew about.

I ask all my terminally ill children whom they would love to see the most, whom they would love to have by their side always, meaning here and now. (By the way many of my adult patients are nonbelieving people, and I could not talk to them about life after death. I do not impose that onto my patients.) So I always ask my children, who would you like to have with you always, if you could choose one person? Ninety-nine percent of the children, except for black children, name mommy and daddy. (With black children, it is very often aunties or grandmas, because aunty or grandma are the ones who love them perhaps the most, or have the most time with them. But those are only cultural differences.) Most of the children say mommy and daddy, but not one of these children who nearly died has ever seen mommy and daddy at this time unless their parents had preceded them in death.

Many people say, well, this is a projection of wishful thinking. Somebody who dies is desperate, lonely, frightened, so they imagine somebody with them who they love. If this were true, ninety-nine percent of all my dying children, my five-, six-, and seven-year-olds, would see their mommies and their daddies. But not one of these children, in all these years that we have collected cases, saw their mommies and daddies because their mommies and daddies were still alive. The factors determining who you see are that the person must have passed on before you, even if only by one minute, and you must have genuinely loved them. This means many of my children see Jesus. A Jewish boy would not see Jesus, because a Jewish boy normally doesn't love Jesus. But these are only religious differences.

I have not finished telling you the story of Mrs. Schwarz. She died two weeks after her son was of age. She was buried (she was one of many patients of mine), and I'm sure I would have forgotten her if she had not visited me again.

Approximately ten months after she was dead and buried, I was in trouble. I'm always in trouble, but at that time I was in bigger trouble. My seminar on Death and Dying had started to deteriorate. The minister I had worked with, and who I loved very dearly, had left. The new minister was very conscious of publicity, and it became an accredited course. Every week we had to talk about the same stuff, and it was like the famous dating show. It wasn't worth it. It was like prolonging life when it's no longer worth living. It was something that was not me, and I decided that the only way that I could stop it was to physically leave the University. Naturally my heart was broken because I really loved this work, but not that way.

So I made the heroic decision that: "I'm going to leave the University of Chicago. Today, immediately after my Death and Dying seminar, I'm going to give notice."

The minister and I had a ritual. After the seminar we would go to the elevator, I would wait for his elevator to come, we would finish business talk, he would leave, and I would go back to my office which was on the same floor at the end of a long hallway. The minister's biggest problem was that he couldn't listen; that was just another of my grievances. And so, between the classroom and the elevator, I tried three times to tell him that it's all his, that I'm leaving. He didn't hear me. He kept talking about something else. I got very desperate, and when I'm desperate I become very active. Before the elevator arrived — he was a huge guy — I grabbed his collar and said, "You are gonna stay right here. I have made a horribly important decision, and I want you to know what it is." I really felt like a hero to be able to do that. He didn't say anything.

At this moment a woman appeared in front of the elevator. I stared at this woman. I cannot tell you how this woman looked, but you can imagine what it's like when you see somebody that you know terribly well, but you suddenly block out who it is. I said to him, "God, who is that? I know that woman, and she's staring at me; she's just waiting until you go into the elevator, and then she'll come." I was so preoccupied with who she was I forgot that I tried to grab him. She stopped that. She was very transparent, but not transparent enough that you could see very much behind her. I asked him once more, but he didn't tell me who she was, so I gave up on him. The last thing I said to him was kind of, "To heck, I'm going over and tell her I just cannot remember her name." That was my last thought before he left.

The moment he had entered the elevator, this woman walked straight towards me and said, "Dr. Ross, I had to come back. Do you mind if I walk you to your office? It will only take two minutes." Something like this. And because she knew where my office was, and she knew my name, I felt kind of safe, I didn't have to admit that I didn't know who she was. This was the longest walk of my life. I am a psychiatrist. I work with schizophrenic patients all the time, and I love them. When they would have visual hallucinations I would tell them, "I know you see that Madonna on the wall, but I don't see it." Now I said to myself, "Elisabeth, I know you see this woman, but that can't be."

All the way from the elevator to my office I did reality testing on myself. I said, "I'm tired, I need a vacation. I think I've seen too many schizophrenic patients. I'm beginning to see things. I have to touch her, to know if she's real." I even touched her skin to see if it was cold or warm, or if the skin would disappear when I touched it. It was the most incredible walk I have ever taken, not knowing why I was doing what I was doing. I was both an observing psychiatrist and a patient. I was everything at one time. I didn't know why I did what I did, or who I thought she was. I even repressed the thought that this could actually be Mrs. Schwarz, who had died and was buried months ago.

When we reached my door she opened it with this incredible kindness and tenderness and love, and she said, "Dr. Ross, I had to come back for two reasons. One, to thank you and Reverend Gaines . . ." (he was a beautiful black minister with whom I had a super, ideal symbiosis), "to thank you and him for what you did for me. But the other reason I had to come back is that you cannot stop this work on death and dying, not yet."

I looked at her, and I don't know if I thought by then, "It could be Mrs. Schwarz," I mean, this woman had been buried for ten months, and I didn't believe in all that stuff. I finally got to my desk. I touched everything that was real. I touched my pen, my desk, my chair, and it's real. I was hoping that she would disappear. But she didn't. She just stood there and stubbornly, but lovingly, said, "Dr. Ross, do you hear me? Your work is not finished. We will help you, and you will know when the time is right, but do not stop now. Promise?"

I thought, "My God, nobody would ever believe me if I told them this, not even my dearest friend." Little did I know I would later tell this to several hundred people. Then the scientist in me won, and I said something very shrewd and a big fat lie. I said to her, "You know Reverend Gaines is in Urbana now." (This was true; he had taken over a church there.) I said, "He would just love to have a note from you. Would you mind?" And I gave her a piece of paper and a pencil. You understand, I had no intention of sending this note to my friend, but I needed scientific proof. I mean, somebody who's buried can't write little love letters. And this woman, with the most human, no, not human, most loving smile, knowing every thought I had — and I knew, it was thought transference if I've ever experienced it — took the paper and wrote a note. Then she said (but without words), "Are you satisfied now?" I looked at her and thought, I will never be able to share this with anybody, but I am going to really hold onto this. Then she got up, ready to leave, repeating: "Dr. Ross, you promise," implying not to give up this work yet. I said, "I promise." And the moment I said, "I promise," she disappeared.

We still have the note.

I was told a year and a half ago that my work with dying patients is finished — there are many others who can carry on now — that this was not my real job, the reason I'm on the earth. The work with death and dying was simply a testing ground for me, to see if I can take hardship, abuse, and resistance. And I passed the test. The second test was to see if I could handle fame. And that didn't affect me, so I passed that too.

But my *real* job is, and this is why I need your help, to tell people that death does not exist. It is very important that mankind knows this, for we are at the beginning of a very difficult time. Not only for this country, but for the whole planet earth. Because of our own destructiveness. Because of nuclear weapons. Because of our greediness and materialism. Because we are piggish in terms of ecology, because we have destroyed so many, many natural resources, and because we have lost all genuine spirituality. I'm exaggerating, but not too much. The only thing that will bring about the change into a new age is that the earth is shaken, that we are shaken, and we are going to be shaken. We have already seen the beginning of it. You have to know not to be afraid. Only if you keep a very, very open channel, an open mind and no fear, will great insight and revelations come to you. They can happen to all of you. You do not have to have a guru, you do not have to go to India, you don't even have to take a TM course. You don't have to do anything except learn to get in touch, in silence, within yourself. Get in touch with your own inner self and learn not to be afraid. One way to not be afraid is to know that death does not exist, that everything in this life has a positive purpose. Get rid of all your negativity and begin to view life as a challenge, a testing ground of your own inner resources and strength.

There are no coincidences. God is not a punitive, nasty God. After you make the transition, then you come to what has been described as hell and heaven.

What we hear from our friends who have passed over, people who came back to share with us, is that every human being, after this transition, is going to have to face something that looks very much like a television screen. You will be given an opportunity — not to be judged by a judgmental God — but to judge yourself, by having to review every single action, every word and every thought of your life. You make your own hell or your own heaven by the way you have lived.

# LIFE, DEATH, AND
# LIFE AFTER DEATH

This is your promised tape on life, death, and life after death. I am sharing with you some of the experiences and findings of the last decade, gathered since we started to seriously study the whole issue of death and life after death. After working with dying patients for so many years, it became very evident that in spite of our existence for so many millions of years as human beings we have not yet come to a clear understanding of perhaps the most important question, namely the meaning and purpose of life and death.

I wanted to share with you some of this research on death and life after death. I think the time has come when we are all going to put these findings together in a language that can help people to understand, and also perhaps help them in dealing with, the death of a loved one. Especially the tragic occurrence of a sudden death when we don't quite understand why these tragedies have to happen to us. It is also very important when you try to counsel and help dying people and their families. And the question occurs over and over again, "What is life, what is death, and why do young children — especially young children — have to die?"

We have not published any of our research for many reasons. We have studied near-death experiences for decades, but we were very aware that those were only "near-death" experiences. We could not share half-truths, we also wanted to know what would happen to those people after they made the transition. The only thing Shanti Nilaya has published so far is a letter that I wrote and illustrated in response to a nine-year-old boy with cancer who lived in the southern part of the United States. He wrote me to ask a very moving question: "What is life and what is death and why do young children have to die?"

I borrowed my daughter's colored felt pencils and printed him a little illustrated letter in simple language that could be understood by any child from pre-school age to early grade school age. His response was not only very positive but, needless to say, he was a very proud young man to have a special little picture book from me. He shared it not only with his parents, but also with the parents of other dying children. As a special gift to me, he gave us permission to have it printed and make it available through Shanti Nilaya to help other young children to understand this most important question. (If you are interested in obtaining a copy, write to Shanti Nilaya and ask for *Letter to a Child with Cancer.*)

A long time ago, people were much more in touch with the issue of death and believed in heaven or life after death. It is only in the last hundred years, perhaps, that fewer and fewer people truly know that life exists after the physical body dies. We are now in a new age, and hopefully we have made a transition from an age of science and technology and materialism to a new age of genuine and authentic spirituality. This does not mean religiosity, but rather, spirituality. Spirituality is an awareness that there is something far greater than we are, something that created this universe, created life, and that we are an authentic, important, significant part of it, and can contribute to its evolution.

All of us when we were born from the Source, from God, were endowed with a facet of divinity. That means, in a very literal sense, that we have a part of that source within us. That is what gives us the knowledge of our immortality. Many people are beginning to be aware that the physical body is only the house or the temple, or as we call it the cocoon, which we inhabit for a certain number of months or years until we make the transition called death. Then, at the time of death, we shed this cocoon and are once again as free as a butterfly to use the symbolic language that we use when talking to dying children and their siblings.

I have worked with dying patients for the last twenty years. When I started this work, I must say, I was neither very interested in life after death nor did I have any really clear picture about the definition of death. When you study the scientific definition of death, you see that it only includes the death of a physical body as if man would only exist as the cocoon. I was one of the physicians and scientists who did not ever question that. It only became a really relevant and important issue in the 60s when the transplant of organs, especially kidneys and hearts, raised an important question as to when are we ethically, morally and legally allowed to remove an organ out of a patient in order to save another person's life. It has become a major legal issue in the last few decades since materialism has reached a point where people sue each other when the issue of prolonging life is raised. We can now be sued for either attempting removal of an organ too early, when a family claims the patient was still alive, or when we wait too long and perhaps prolong a life unnecessarily. The insurance companies have added to this problem. In a family accident it is sometimes of vital importance to know who in the family died before, even if by only minutes. Again, the issue is money, and who would benefit. Needless to say, all these issues would have touched me very little had it not been for my own very subjective experiences at the bedsides of my own dying patients.

Being a skeptical semi-believer, to put it mildly, and not interested in issues of life after death, I could not help but be impressed by several observations which occurred so frequently that I began to wonder why nobody ever studied the real issues of death. Not for any special scientific reasons, not to cover lawsuits, needless to say, but simply out of natural curiosity.

Man has existed for forty-seven million years and has been in its present existence, which includes the facet of divinity, for seven million years. Every day people die all over the world. Yet in a society that is able to send a man to the moon and bring him back well and safe, we have never put any effort into the definition of human death. Isn't that peculiar?

So in the midst of caring for dying patients and the teaching of medical and seminary students, we decided one day on the spur of the moment that we would try to come up with a new, updated, all-inclusive definition of death. It is said somewhere: "Ask and you will be given, knock and the door will be opened." Or in another way: "A teacher will appear when the student is ready."

This proved to be very true one week after raising this important question and making a commitment to finding an answer. We were visited by nurses who shared with us the experiences of a woman who had been in the intensive care unit fifteen times. Each time this woman was expected to die, yet each time she was able to walk out of the intensive care unit to live for another few weeks or months. She was, as we would call it now, our first example of near-death experience.

This occurred at the same time as my increasing sensitivity and observation of other unexplained phenomena at the time when my patients were very, very close to death. Many of them began to hallucinate the presence of loved ones with whom they apparently had some form of communication, but who I personally was neither able to see nor hear. I was also quite aware that even the angriest and most difficult patients, very shortly before death, began to relax deeply, to have a sense of serenity around them. And they were pain free, in spite of having a cancer-filled body. Also, the moment after death occurred, their facial features showed an incredible sense of peace, equanimity and serenity which I could not comprehend since it was often a death that occurred in a state of anger, bargaining, or depression.

My third and perhaps most subjective observation was the fact that I had always been very close to my patients and allowed myself to get deeply and lovingly involved with them. They touched my life — I touched their lives — in a very intimate, meaningful way. Yet within minutes after their death, I had no feelings for these patients, and often wondered if there was something wrong with me. When I looked at them, they appeared similar to a winter coat to be shed with the occurrence of spring, knowing it isn't needed anymore. I had this incredibly clear image of a shell, and my beloved patient was no longer in that "shell."

Naturally, as a scientist, I could not explain this so I would have put these observations aside if it had not been for Mrs. Schwarz. Her husband was a known schizophrenic and each time he had a psychotic episode he would try to kill his youngest son, the youngest of many children and the only one still at home. Mrs. Schwarz was convinced that if she should die prematurely, her husband would lose control and the life of her youngest son would be in danger. Through the help of the Legal Aid Society, we were able to make arrangements for her to transfer the custody of this child to some relatives. She left the hospital with a great sense of relief and a new freedom, knowing that should she not be able to live at least her youngest child was now safe.

It was this same patient who returned to our hospital almost a year later and shared her near-death experience. Experiences like this have been published in many books and magazines in the last few years and have become familiar to the general public, but our first experience was with Mrs. Schwarz who told of having been hospitalized on an emergency basis in a local hospital in Indiana. At the time, being too sick to be transferred as far as Chicago, she remembers being admitted in critical condition. She was put into a private room in a hospital and just as she was contemplating whether she should struggle once more for the sake of the youngest child or simply let go, lean back in a pillow and shed her cocoon, she became aware of a nurse who walked into the room, took one look at her, and dashed out. At that very moment she saw herself slowly and peacefully floating out of her physical body, hovering a few feet above her bed. She even had a great sense of humor, relating that she "looked at" her body which looked pale and icky. She had a sense of awe and surprise, but no fear or anxiety. She then told of watching the resuscitation team walk into the room, enumerating in great detail who walked in first, who walked in last. She was totally aware of every word of their conversations, of their thought patterns, and she had only one great need, to convey to them to relax, to take it easy, and to tell them that she was all right. But the more desperately she tried to convey this to them, the more frantically they seemed to work on her body. Finally it dawned on her that she was able to perceive them but they were not able to perceive her. Mrs. Schwarz then decided to give up her attempts, and in her own language she said: "I lost consciousness." She was declared dead after 45 minutes of unsuccessful resuscitation attempts, but later on showed signs of life again, much to the surprise of the hospital staff. She lived another year-and-a-half. Mrs. Schwarz shared this with my class and myself in one of my seminars.

Needless to say, this was a brand new experience for me. I had never heard of near-death experiences, in spite of the fact that I had been a physician for many years. My students were shocked that I did not call this hallucination and illusion, or a feeling of depersonalization. They had a desperate need to give it a label — something that they could identify — and then put it aside and not have to deal with it.

Mrs. Schwarz's experience, we were sure, could not be a single, unique occurrence. Our hope was to be able to find more cases like hers, and perhaps move in the direction of collecting data to see if this was a common, rare, or very unique experience. It has become known recently that many, many researchers, physicians, psychologists and people who study parapsychological phenomena have tried to collect cases like this. In the last ten years, over twenty-five thousand cases have been collected from all over the world.

It may be simplest to summarize what many of these cases show people experience at the moment of cessation of physical bodily functioning. We call these near-death experiences, and all of these patients have made a comeback and were able to share with us after they recovered. We will talk later about what happens to those who do not make a comeback. It is important to understand that of the many people who have cardiac arrest or are resuscitated, only one out of ten has a conscious recollection of their experiences during this temporary cessation of vital functions. This is very understandable if we compare it with the average population. All of you dream every night, but only a small percentage are aware of their dreams on awakening.

The cases we collected are not only from the United States, but also from Australia, Canada, and other countries. The youngest involves a two-year-old child, the oldest a ninety-seven-year-old man. We studied people from different cultural and religious backgrounds, including Eskimos, original Hawaiians, Aboriginals from Australia, Hindus, Buddhists, Protestants, Catholics, Jews and several people without any religious identification including a few who call themselves agnostics or atheists. It was important for us to collect data from the greatest possible variety of people from different religious and cultural backgrounds. We wanted to be very sure that our material was not contaminated, and that it was a uniquely human experience having nothing to do with early religious or other conditioning.

We can say, after all these years of collecting data, that the following points are common denominators in all those cases of people who have had a near-death experience. Also relevant is the fact that they had these experiences after an accident, murder attempt, suicide attempt, or a slow lingering death. Over half of our cases have been sudden death experiences, therefore the patients would have not been able to prepare or anticipate an experience. At the moment of death, all of you will experience the separation of the real immortal You, from the temporary house, namely the physical body. We will call this immortal self the soul or the entity, or using the symbolic language that we use when we communicate with children, we call it the butterfly in the process of leaving the cocoon. When we leave the physical body there will be a total absence of panic, fear or anxiety. We will always experience a physical wholeness and will be totally aware of the environment in which this accident or death occurs. This may be a hospital room, our own bedroom after experiencing a coronary attack at home, or after a tragic car accident or a plane crash. We will be quite aware of the people who work with the resuscitation team, or the people who work in a rescue attempt to extricate a mutilated and hurt body from a car wreck. We will watch this at the distance of a few feet, in a rather detached state of mind, if I may use the word mind, though we are no longer connected with the mind or functioning brain at this moment in most cases.

This all occurs at the time when we have no measurable signs of brain activity. It happens very often at the time when physicians find no signs of life whatsoever. At this moment of observation of the scene of death we will be aware of people's conversation, their behavior, their attire and their thoughts without having any negative feelings about the whole occurrence.

Our second body, which we experience at this time, is not the physical body but an ethereal body. (We will talk later on about the differences between physical, psychic and spiritual energy which create these forms.) In the second, temporary, ethereal body we experience a total wholeness as I said before. If we have been amputees, we will have our legs again. If we have been deaf mutes, we can hear and talk and sing. If we have been a multiple-sclerosis patient in a wheelchair with blurred vision, blurred speech and unable to move our legs, we are able to sing and dance again.

It is understandable that many of our patients who have been successfully resuscitated are not always grateful when their butterfly is squashed back into the cocoon, since with the revival of our bodily functions we also have to accept the pains and the handicaps that go with it. In the state of the ethereal body, we have no pain and no handicaps.

Many of my colleagues wondered if this is not simply projection of our wishful thinking, which could be very understandable and comprehensible. If anyone has been paralyzed, mute, blind or handicapped for many, many years, they may be looking forward to a time when their suffering is ended.

It is very easy to evaluate whether this is a projection of wishful thinking or not. Half of our cases have been sudden, unexpected accidents or near-death experiences where people who were unable to foresee what was going to hit them, as in the case of a hit-and-run driver who amputated the legs of one of our patients. When the patient was out of his physical body, he saw his amputated legs on a highway, yet he was fully aware of having both of his legs on his ethereal, perfect and whole body. We cannot assume that he had previous knowledge of the loss of his legs and would therefore project in his own wishful thinking that he would be able to walk again.

But there is a much simpler way to rule out the projection of wishful thinking, and that is to study blind people who do not have light perception. We asked them to share with us what it was like when they had this near-death experience. If it was just wish fulfillment, these blind people would not be able to share with us the color of a sweater, the design of a tie, or many details of shape, colors and designs of people's clothing. We have questioned several totally blind people and they were not only able to tell us who came into the room first and who worked on the resuscitation, but they were able to give minute details of the attire and the clothing of all the people present, something a totally blind person would never be able to do.

Besides the absence of pain and the experience of a physical wholeness in a simulated perfect body, which we may call the ethereal body, people will also be aware that it is impossible to die alone. There are three reasons why no one can die alone. By no one I mean even people who would die in a desert a few hundred miles away from the nearest human being, or an astronaut who would be sent alone into the universe, miss the target and circle around the universe until he died of natural causes.

When slowly preparing for death, as is often the case with children who have cancer, prior to death many of these children begin to be aware that they have the ability to leave their physical body and have what we call an out-of-body experience. All of us have these out-of-body experiences during certain stages of sleep. Very few of us are consciously aware of it. Dying children especially, who are much more tuned in, become more spiritual than healthy children of the same age. They become aware of these short trips out of their physical bodies which help them in the transition, which help them familiarize themselves with the place they are going to.

It is during these out-of-body trips which dying patients, young and old, experience that they become aware of the presence of beings who surround them, who guide them and who help them. Young children often refer to them as their playmates. The churches have called them guardian angels. Most researchers would call them guides. It is not important what label we give them, but it is important to know that every single human being, from the moment of birth until the moment when we make the transition and end this physical existence, is in the presence of these guides or guardian angels who will wait for us and help us in the transition from life to life after death. Also, we will always be met by those who preceded us in death who we have loved.

The third reason we cannot die alone is that when we shed our physical bodies, even temporarily, prior to death, we are in an existence where there is no time and no space. In this existence we can be anywhere we choose to be at the speed of our thoughts.

Little Susy, who is dying of leukemia in a hospital, may be attended by her mother for weeks and weeks. It becomes very clear to the dying child that it is increasingly difficult for her to leave mommy who sometimes implicitly or explicitly conveys: "Honey, don't die on me, I can't live without you." So, what we are doing to those patients, is to make them, in a sense, guilty for dying on us. Susy, who has become more and more tuned in with total life, has the awareness of her existence after death and the full awareness of a continuation of life. Susy, during the night and during normal state of consciousness has been out of her body and is aware of her ability to travel and to literally fly anywhere she wants to be. She simply asks mommy to leave the hospital. Often children say: "Mommy you look so tired, why don't you go home, take a shower, take a rest. I am really okay now." The mother leaves, and half-an-hour later the nurse may call from the hospital and say: "I'm sorry, Mrs. Smith, your daughter just passed away."

Unfortunately, those parents are often left with a tremendous amount of guilt and shame and reprimand themselves for not having stuck it out so they would have been with their child at the moment of death. They do not understand or comprehend that no one can die alone. Susy, unburdened of their needs, is able to let go of the cocoon and free herself quite quickly. She will then, at the speed of her thoughts, be with mommy or daddy or whoever she needs to be with.

We have all been endowed by a facet of divinity. We received this gift seven million years ago, and it includes not only the ability to exercise free choice, but also the ability to shed our physical body — not only at the time of death but in times of crisis, in times of exhaustion, in times of very extraordinary circumstances, and during a certain type of sleep. It is important to know this can happen before death.

Victor Frankl, in his very beautiful book, *The Search for Meaning*, wrote of his experiences in the concentration camps. He was probably one of the best known scientists who studied out-of-body experiences many decades ago when it was not yet popular. He studied people who fell from the mountains in Europe, whose experiences went through their minds during the very brief period of maybe a few seconds during a fall, and he became aware that during this out-of-body experience time cannot possibly exist. Many people have had similar experiences with nearly drowning, or during a time of their lives when they were in great danger.

Our study was verified by laboratory research with the collaboration of Robert Monroe who wrote the book *Journeys Out of the Body*. We have studied spontaneous out-of-body experiences as well as those induced in a laboratory supervised by Monroe and watched, observed and shared by several scientists from the Menninger Foundation in Topeka. More and more scientists and researchers are repeating this kind of study now, and have found it to be quite verifiable. Naturally, it lends itself to many aspects of the study of a dimension which is very hard to conceive of with our three-dimensional scientific approach to life.

We have also been questioned about the guides or guardian angels, about the presence of loving human beings, especially deceased members of the family who preceded one in death, and who come and welcome us at the time of transition. Again, the question comes up naturally: how do you verify such frequent occurrences in a more scientific way?

It is interesting to me as a psychiatrist that thousands of people all around the globe should share the same "hallucinations" prior to death, namely the awareness of some relatives or friends who preceded them in death.

There must be some explanation for this. So we proceeded, trying to find ways to study this, to verify this, or perhaps to verify that this is simply a projection of wishful thinking.

Perhaps the best way to study this is to sit with dying children after family accidents. We would usually do this after Fourth of July weekends, Memorial Day or Labor Day, times when families go out together and all too often have head-on collisions which kill some members of the family and bring many injured survivors into hospitals. I have made it a task to sit with the critically injured children since they are my specialty. I am aware that they have not been informed that any of their relatives have been killed. I am always impressed that they are aware of those who preceded them in death. I sit with them, watch them silently, perhaps hold their hand. I watch their restlessness, but often, shortly prior to death, a peaceful serenity overtakes them, an ominous sign. It is at this time that I ask them if they are willing and able to share with me what they are experiencing. They share in very similar words, "Everything is all right now. Mommy and Peter are already waiting for me." I am aware that the mother was killed, suddenly, at the scene of the accident. But I am not aware that her brother Peter also died. Shortly afterwards, I receive a phone call from the children's hospital that Peter had died ten minutes ago.

In all the many years that we have collected this kind of data, we have never met a child who in the imminence of their own death mentioned a person in their family that had not preceded them in death, even if by only a few minutes. I do not know how to explain this, except from the knowledge that these children are already aware of the presence of their family members who will wait for them for the time of their own transition. Then they are reunited in a different form of life that many people do not comprehend.

Another experience moved me even more than the children's. It was the case of an American Indian. To date we have very little data since American Indians do not often talk about issues of death and dying. This young American Indian woman was struck by a hit-and-run driver on a highway. A stranger had stopped his car in an attempt to help her. She calmly told him that there was nothing else he could do for her, except one day he might get near the Indian reservation where her mother lived — about seven hundred miles away from the scene of the accident. She had a message for her mother, and maybe one day he would be able to convey this message to her. The message stated that she was okay. That she was not only okay, that she was very happy because she was already together with her dad. She died in the arms of this stranger, who was so touched that he was there at the right time and place that he drove seven hundred miles out of his way to visit the mother. When he arrived at the Indian reservation, he was told that her mate, the victim's father, had died one hour prior to the daughter's accident of a coronary.

We have many, many cases like this where someone was dying and had not been informed or aware of the death of a family member, and yet were greeted by them. We became aware that their job was not to convince or to convert others of the fact that death does not exist, but simply to share. If you are ready to hear it, and willing to have an open mind, you will get and find your own experiences. They are easy to have if you ask for it.

In every audience of eight hundred people there are at least twelve authentic cases of people who have had such an experience and who are willing to share it. You must be able to have an open mind and not be critical, negative, judgmental or have a need to label it with a psychiatric label. The only thing that prevents these people from sharing their experience with others in our society is our incredible tendency to label, to belittle, or to deny such stories when they make us uncomfortable and don't fit into our own scientific or religious model. All the experiences I have shared so far will be the experiences you have when you are in a critical condition, or near death. Needless to say, all the people who shared those experiences with us have been people who made a comeback.

My most dramatic and unforgettable case of "ask and you will be given," and also of a near-death experience, was a man who was in the process of being picked up by his entire family for a Memorial Day weekend drive to visit some relatives out of town. While driving in the family van to pick him up, his parents-in-law with his wife and eight children were hit by a gasoline tanker. The gasoline poured over the car and burned his entire family to death. After being told what happened, this man remained in a state of total shock and numbness for several weeks. He stopped working and was unable to communicate. To make a long story short, he became a total bum, drinking half-a-gallon of whisky a day, trying heroin and other drugs to numb his pain. He was unable to hold a job for any length of time and ended up literally in the gutter.

It was during one of my hectic traveling tours, having just finished the second lecture in a day on life after death, that a hospice group in Santa Barbara asked me to give yet another lecture. After my preliminary statements, I became aware that I am very tired of repeating the same stories over and over again. And I quietly said to myself: "Oh God, why don't you send me somebody from the audience who has had a near-death experience and is willing to share it with the audience so I can take a break? They will have a first-hand experience instead of hearing my old stories over and over again."

At that very moment the organizer of the group gave me a little slip of paper with an urgent message on it. It was a message from a man from the bowery who begged to share his near-death experience with me. I took a little break and sent a messenger to his bowery hotel. A few moments later, after a speedy cab ride, the man appeared in the audience. Instead of being a bum as he had described himself, he was a rather well dressed, very sophisticated man. He went up on the stage and without having a need to evaluate him, I encouraged him to tell the audience what he needed to share.

He told how he had been looking forward to the weekend family reunion, how his entire family had piled into a family van and were on the way to pick him up when this tragic accident occurred which burned his entire family to death. He shared the shock and the numbness, the utter disbelief of suddenly being a single man, of having had children and suddenly becoming childless, of living without a single close relative. He told of his total inability to come to grips with it. He shared how he changed from a money-earning, decent, middle-class husband and father to a total bum, drunk every day from morning to night, using every conceivable drug and trying to commit suicide in every conceivable way, yet never able to succeed. His last recollection was that after two years of literally bumming around, he was lying on a dirt road at the edge of a forest, drunk and stoned as he called it, trying desperately to be reunited with his family. Not wanting to live, not even having the energy to move out of the road when he saw a big truck coming toward him and running over him.

It was at this moment that he watched himself in the street, critically injured, while he observed the whole scene of the accident from a few feet above. It was at this moment that his family appeared in front of him, in a glow of light with an incredible sense of love. They had happy smiles on their faces, and simply made him aware of their presence, not communicating in any verbal way but in the form of thought transference, sharing with him the joy and happiness of their present existence.

This man was not able to tell us how long this reunion lasted. He was so awed by his family's health, their beauty, their radiance and their total acceptance of this present situation, by their unconditional love. He made a vow not to touch them, not to join them, but to re-enter his physical body so that he could share with the world what he had experienced. It would be a form of redemption for his two years of trying to throw his physical life away. It was after this vow that he watched the truck driver carry his totally injured body into the car. He saw an ambulance speeding to the scene of the accident, he was taken to the hospital's emergency room and he finally re-entered his physical body, tore off the straps that were tied around him and literally walked out the emergency room. He never had delirium tremens or any aftereffects from the heavy abuse of drugs and alcohol. He felt healed and whole, and made a commitment that he would not die until he had the opportunity of sharing the existence of life after death with as many people as would be willing to listen. It was after reading a newspaper article about my appearance in Santa Barbara that he sent a message to the auditorium. By allowing him to share with my audience he was able to keep the promise he made at the time of his short, temporary, yet happy reunion with his entire family.

We do not know what happened to this man since then, but I will never forget the glow in his eyes, the joy and deep gratitude he experienced that he was led to a place where, without doubt and questioning, he was allowed to stand up on the stage and share with a group of hundreds of hospice workers the total knowledge and awareness that our physical body is only the shell that encloses our immortal self.

The next question, naturally, is: "What happens, then, after death?" We have studied very young children who have not yet read books or magazine articles, or listened to accounts of others like this man. Yet even our youngest patient, a two-year-old child, was able to share with us what he experienced and called the moment of death. The only difference between people from different religious backgrounds is the presence of certain religious figures, and the two-year-old is perhaps our best example. He had an anaphylactic allergic reaction to a drug given to him by a physician and was declared dead. While the physician and his mother waited for the arrival of the father, the mother desperately touched her little boy, crying, sobbing and pleading with him. After what seemed to her an eternity, her little two-year-old opened his eyes and said in the voice of a wise old man: "Mommy, I was with Jesus and with Mary. Mary kept telling me that my time was not right, I had to go back. I tried to ignore her, and she realized that I was trying to ignore her. She pulled me gently by the wrist and took me away from Jesus and said: 'You have to get back, Peter. You have to save your mommy from the fire.'" It was at this moment that Peter opened his eyes and said in a happy voice: "You know, mommy, when she told me that I ran all the way back home."

This mother was not able to share this incident for thirteen years, and was rather depressed because of the misinterpretation of Mary's statement to her son Peter. Her misunderstanding was that her son was eventually the one who had to save her from the fire, from hell, and she couldn't understand why she was doomed to hell. She was a very decent, hard-working woman of faith. I tried to convey to her that she did not understand the symbolic language, that this was a unique and beautiful gift of Mary who is, like all beings in a spiritual realm, a being of total and unconditional love, unable to condemn or to criticize. I asked her for a moment to stop thinking and to simply allow her own spiritual intuitive quadrant to respond. I asked her: "What would it have been like if Mary had not sent Peter back to you thirteen years ago?" She grabbed her hair and she shouted out: "Oh my god, I would have gone through hell and fire." Needless to say, it was no longer important to point out: "Now do you understand that Mary saved you from the fire?"

The scriptures are full of examples of symbolic language. If people would listen more to their own intuitive spiritual quadrant and not contaminate their understanding of these beautiful messages with their own negativity, their own fears, their own guilts, their own needs to punish others or themselves, they would begin to comprehend the beautiful symbolic language that dying patients use when they try to convey to us their needs, their knowledge and their awareness.

A Jewish child would not be likely to see Jesus, a Protestant child would not likely see Mary, not that they would not care for those children but simply because we always get what we need the most. The ones we meet are the ones we have loved the most and who preceded us in death.

After we are met by those we have loved, after we are met by our own guides and guardian angels, we are passing through a symbolic transition often described as a tunnel. Some people experience it as a river, some as a gate; each one will choose what is most symbolically appropriate. In my own personal experience it was a mountain pass with wild flowers simply because my concept of heaven includes mountains and wild flowers, the source of much happiness in my childhood in Switzerland. This is culturally determined.

After we pass through this visually very beautiful and individually appropriate form of transition, say the tunnel, we are approaching a source of light that many of our patients describe and that I myself experienced in the form of an incredibly beautiful and unforgettable life changing experience. This is called cosmic consciousness. In the presence of this light, which most people in our western hemisphere called Christ or God, or love, or light, we are surrounded by total and absolute unconditional love, understanding and compassion. This light is a source of pure spiritual energy and no longer physical or psychic energy. (Spiritual energy can neither be manipulated nor used by human beings.) It is an energy in the realm of existence, where negativity is impossible. This means that no matter how bad we have been in our life, or how guilty we feel, we are unable to experience any negative emotions. It is also totally impossible to be condemned in this presence, which many people call Christ or God, since He is a being of total and absolute unconditional love. It is in this presence that we become aware of our potential, of what we could be like, of what we could have lived like. It is also in this presence, surrounded by compassion, love and understanding, that we are asked to review and evaluate our total existence since we are no longer attached to our mind or physical brain and our limiting physical body. We have all-knowledge and all-understanding. It is in this existence that we have to review and evaluate every thought, every word and every deed of our existence. And we will be simultaneously aware of how we have affected others. In the presence of spiritual energy we no longer have the need for a physical form. We leave this ethereal simulated body behind and resume again the form that we had before we were born, and the form we will have when we merge with the source, with God, when we have finished our destiny.

It is important to understand that from the moment of our existence until we return to God, we always maintain our own identity and our own energy pattern. In the billions of people in this universe, on this physical planet and in the unobstructed world, there are not two of the same energy patterns, no two people alike (not even identical twins!). If anybody doubts the greatness of our creator, one should consider what genius it takes to create billions of energy patterns, no two alike. This is the uniqueness of the human being. I could only compare this miracle to the number of snowflakes on this planet earth, knowing that there are not two snowflakes alike. I have had the great blessing of being able to see with my own physical eyes the presence of hundreds of those energy patterns in full daylight, and it is very similar to a fluttering, pulsating series of different snowflakes all with their different lights, their different colors and their different forms and shapes. This is what we are like after we die. This is also how we existed before we were born.

It takes up no space, no time, to go from one star to another, from planet earth to another galaxy. And those energy patterns of those beings are with us right here. If we only had the eyes to see it, we would be aware that we are never ever alone. We are surrounded by these beings who guide us, who love us, who protect us, who try to direct us, to help us follow the track that will fulfill our destiny. Maybe in times of great pain, of great sorrow and great loneliness, we can get tuned in and become aware of their presence. We can ask them to make their presence known to us. We can ask them questions before we are asleep, and we can ask them to give us an answer in our dreams. Those who have been tuned in to their sleep states, to their dreams, become aware that many of our questions are answered in this state. As we get more tuned in to our own inner entity, to our own inner spiritual part, it is very understandable that we can get help and guidance from our own all-knowing self, that immortal part we call the butterfly.

L et me share with you some of my own mystical experiences that helped me to truly *know* rather than just believe that all these existences beyond the realm of our scientific understanding are true, are reality, are something available to all human beings. I have to make it very clear that in my early years I had no comprehension of higher consciousness. I never had a guru, in fact I was never really able to meditate, a source of great peace and understanding for many people not only in the eastern hemisphere but more and more in the western world. It is true that I am getting totally tuned in when I communicate with dying patients. And maybe in those thousands of hours that I have been sitting with them where nothing and no one was able to distract us, this might be considered a form of meditation. If that is true, then I have indeed meditated for many, many hours. But I truly believe that it is not necessary to go to a mountain top, to live as a hermit, or to go to India to find a guru in order to have these mystical experiences.

I truly believe that every human being consists of a physical, an emotional, an intellectual and a spiritual quadrant. If we can learn to externalize our unnatural emotions, our hate, our anguish, our unresolved grief, our oceans of unshed tears, then we can get back, get tuned in to what we were meant to be: a human being consisting of four quadrants, all of which work together in total harmony and wholeness. It is only if we have learned to accept our physicalness, if we love and accept our physical body, if we are able to share our natural emotions without being handicapped by them, without being belittled when we cry, when we express natural anger, when we are jealous in order to emulate someone else's talents, gifts or behavior. Then we will be able to understand that we have only two natural fears, one of falling and one of loud noises. All other fears have been given to us by grown-ups who projected their own fears onto us, and have passed them on from generation to generation.

Most important of all, we must learn to love and be loved unconditionally. Most of us have been raised as prostitutes. I will love you "if." And this word "if" has ruined and destroyed more lives than anything else on this planet earth. It prostitutes us, it makes us feel that we can buy love with good behavior, or good grades. We will never develop a sense of self-love and self-reward. If we were not able to accommodate the grown-ups, we were punished, rather than being taught by consistent loving discipline. As our teachers taught, if you had been raised with unconditional love and discipline you will never be afraid of the windstorms of life. You would have no fear, no guilt and no anxieties, the only enemies of men. Should you shield the canyon from the windstorms you would never see the beauty of their carvings.

And so I went about — not looking for a guru, not trying to meditate, not trying to reach any state of higher consciousness. But each time a patient or a life situation made me aware of some negativity within me, I tried to externalize it so I would eventually reach that harmony between my physical, emotional, spiritual and intellectual quadrants. As I did my homework and tried to practice what I go around teaching, I was blessed with more and more mystical experiences, getting in touch with my own intuitive spiritual all-knowing and all-understanding self. But I was also able to get in touch with the guidance which comes from the unobstructed world, and which always surrounds us and waits for an occasion, an opportunity to not only impinge on us knowledge and direction, but also to help us understand what life, and especially our own personal destiny, is all about. This is so we can fulfill our destiny in one lifetime and do not have to return in order to learn the lessons we have not been able to pass in this existence.

One of my first lessons was during a research project where I had an out-of-body experience, induced by iatrogenic means, in a laboratory in Virginia, observed by several skeptical scientists. It was during one of these out-of-body experiences that I was slowed down by the laboratory chief who felt that I went too fast. Much to my dismay, he interfered with my own needs and my own personality. During a second attempt at having an out-of-body experience, I was determined to circumvent this problem by giving myself a self-induction to go faster than the speed of light and further than any human being has ever gone during an out-of-body experience. The moment the induction was given I literally left my body at an incredible speed.

The only memory I had when I returned into my physical body were the words *Shanti Nilaya*. I had no idea about the meaning and significance of this, and had no concept of where I had been. The only awareness I had was that I was healed of an almost complete bowel obstruction, and also of a very painful slipped disc which made it impossible for me to even pick up a book from the floor. When I came out of this experiment my bowel obstruction was healed, and I was literally able to lift a hundred-pound sugar bag from the floor without any discomfort or pain. I was told that I radiated, that I looked twenty years younger. Everyone present tried to press me for information, but I had no idea where I had been until the night following the experiment. A night spent in a lonely guest-house, alone in the forest of the Blue Ridge Mountains. Gradually, and not without trepidation, the awareness came to me that I had gone too far and that I now had to accept the consequences of my own choices. I tried to fight sleep during that night, having a vague, inner-knowledge that "it" would happen, but not knowing what "it" would mean. And the moment I let go I had probably the most painful, most agonizing experience any human being has ever lived through. I literally experienced the thousand deaths of my thousand patients. It was a total physical, spiritual, emotional, and intellectual agony caus-ing the inability to breathe, a doubling up of my body, an agonizing physical pain and a total knowledge and awareness that I was out of reach of any human being. And I had to somehow make it through that night.

In those agonizing hours I had only three reprieves. It was very similar to labor pains, and after each labor pain another one followed immediately without an instant to breathe in between. In those three brief moments when I was able to catch a breath, there were some significant symbolic occurrences which I understood only much later.

During the first reprieve, I begged for a shoulder to lean on. I literally expected a man's left shoulder to appear so I could put my head on it and bear the agony somewhat better. In the same instance that I asked for the shoulder to lean on, a deep, caring, compassionate and severe voice simply stated: "You shall not be given."

Endless time later, when I had another moment to catch a breath, I begged for a hand to hold. Again, I expected a hand to show up at the right side of my bed, so I could grab onto it and endure the agony somewhat easier. And the same voice spoke again: "You shall not be given."

The third and last time I was able to catch a breath, I contemplated asking for a fingertip. But, very much in character for me, I said: "No, if I can't get the hand I don't want the fingertip either." The meaning of the fingertip was simply the awareness of the presence of a human being, with the full knowledge that I could not hold onto that fingertip. It became, for the first time in my life, an issue of faith. And the faith had something to do with a deep, inner knowledge that I had the strength and the courage to endure this agony by myself. But it also included the faith and the knowledge that we are never given more than we can bear. I suddenly became aware that all I needed to do was to stop my fight, to stop my rebellion, to stop being a warrior and move from rebellion to a simple, peaceful, positive submission — to an ability to simply say "yes" to it.

Once I did that, the agony stopped and my breathing was easier. My physical pain disappeared at the moment I uttered the word "yes," not in words but in thoughts. And instead of the thousand deaths, I lived through a rebirth beyond human description.

It started with a very fast vibration, or pulsation, of my abdominal area which spread through my entire body and then to anything that my eyes could see — the ceiling, the wall, the floors, the furniture, the bed, the window, the horizons outside of my window, the trees, and eventually the whole planet earth. It was as if the whole planet was in a very high speed vibration, every molecule vibrated. At the same time, something that looked like a lotus flower bud appeared and opened into an incredible, beautiful, colorful flower. Behind the lotus flower appeared the light that my patients so often talk about. And as I approached this light through the open lotus flower, with a whirl in a deep, fast vibration, I gradually and slowly merged into this incredible unconditional love, into this light. I became one with it.

At the moment of merging into this source of light, all vibrations stopped. A deep silence came over me, and I fell into a deep trance-like sleep from which I awoke knowing that I had to wear a robe, put my sandals on, and walk down the hill. This would occur at the moment the sun was rising from below the horizon.

Approximately an hour and a half later I woke up, put on my robe and sandals and walked down the hill. I experienced probably the greatest ecstasy of existence that human beings can ever experience on this physical plane. I was in total love and awe of all life around me. I was in love with every leaf, every cloud, every piece of grass, every living creature. I felt the pulsation of the pebbles on the path, and I literally walked above the pebbles, convey-ing to them: "I cannot step on you, I cannot hurt you." As

I reached the bottom of the hill I became aware that I had not touched the ground on this path. Yet, there was no questioning the validity of this experience, it was simply an awareness of a cosmic consciousness of life in every living thing, and of a love that can never ever be described in words.

It took me several days to come back to my physical existence with the trivialities of washing dishes, doing the laundry and cooking a meal for my family. And it took several months before I was able to verbalize my experience and share it with a beautiful, non-judgmental, understanding group, a group who had invited me to speak at a conference on transpersonal psychology in Berkeley, California. After I shared my experience, I was given a label for it. It was called cosmic consciousness. As usual, I had to go to the library to find a book with the same title to learn intellectually, and to comprehend, the meaning of such a state. I was also told at that moment that as I merged into this spiritual energy, the source of all light, the words that were given to me, Shanti Nilaya, mean the final home of peace, the home all of us will return to when we have gone through all the agonies, the pains, the sorrows, the griefs. It is where we will be able to let go of the pain and become what we were created to be, a being of harmony between the physical, the emotional, the intellectual and the spiritual quadrants, a being that understands that love, true love, has no claims and no "ifs." If we could understand this state of love, then all of us would be whole and healthy, and all of us would be able to fulfill our destiny in a single lifetime.

This experience has touched and changed my life in ways that are very difficult to put into words. But I think it was because of this experience that I understood that if I ever shared my understanding of life after death, I would literally have to go through a thousand deaths. The society in which I live would try to shred me to pieces, but the experience and the knowledge, the joy, the love and the sensation of what followed the agony, the rewards would always be far greater than the pain.

# DEATH OF A PARENT

The death of a loved one is always a sad event. The resulting behavior of the next-of-kin depends on many different factors, the age of the deceased, as well as that of the surviving child, is very relevant. The cause and/or suddenness (lack of preparedness) plays an important role. The relationship between the parent and the surviving child, as well as the degree of previous similar events in the child's experiences will all affect the bereavement period which will follow the death of a parent.

If the child is very young and has had little time for bonding with a parental figure, almost any parent substitute like a grandma can relatively easily replace a young mother, and the infant will not suffer or show any signs of mourning — which can only take place when the baby's emotional quadrant has already developed. In the first months of life, the physical needs of the baby are the most important and, as long as they are met with a certain consistency, warmth and love, the baby will be satisfied.

Once the bonding has taken place, a baby deprived of the mother will react with physical symptoms, crying and inability to sleep, clinging to other familiar figures, and a regression into earlier behavior can take place. It is the preschool child who will react worst when a mother and/or father dies suddenly. For such a child, death cannot be perceived as a permanent happening and he/she has no concept of death as a permanent separation. They will look for the missing parent everywhere. They will actually try to bribe them to come back. They may be convinced that they caused the "disappearance" of a mother, sure that mother was angry at them, thus trying to punish them with what they perceive as a temporary disappearing act. They may suddenly become unusually well-behaved, volunteer to wash the dishes, to make a bed, to clean up the dishes — and adults may be impressed by this "helpful little guy" who suddenly becomes such a helpful child. This is ominous behavior as it covers up guilt and fear over earlier real or imagined misbehavior, and is an attempt to appease mommy, to bribe her to come back home. It is important for grown-ups to become aware of this behavior and neither compliment the child too much for "being such a good child," nor discourage them. A repeated statement that one cannot cause mommy's death by thinking or behavior may eventually sink in.

It is only when the surviving parent, or perhaps a grandparent, has had a good talk and a good cry over the death of the child's parent that the child can give himself permission to acknowledge the death of one of the parents and begin the actual mourning process. If families can cry and talk together about the happy memories they share of the much missed person, the real process of bereavement can be greatly enhanced. Every child needs to have someone he can talk to about the person he lost. If relatives can go through the pages of a photograph book and share memories of places, vacations, incidents, and laugh and cry together, much can be done to help the child to get through the mourning process without scars.

A third-grader shared with me her grief over the loss of her mother in a car accident which also killed her three-year-old (and only) brother. Her father was the driver of the vehicle, and he felt extremely guilty about the tragic double-loss which he felt he had caused by not listening to those in the family who had tried to talk him out of the fatal trip.

Susy told me: "I was sick in bed when my dad came in to tell me that a babysitter would arrive shortly to take care of me while he, mom, and Peter would have to be away for a few hours." Susy started sobbing again just as she had a year ago when her father informed her of the planned short trip. "I screamed at dad, telling him that I was sick, that I needed mom at home, that I needed no babysitter . . . but he did not want to hear my objections." "Be a big girl," he said, "we will all be home when you wake up in the morning and by then, hopefully, you will feel better." "No arguing or crying helped. He was determined to drive upstate without giving any reason why this had to be done today of all days. The doctor had been in earlier and told my parents to keep me in bed and under observation, as he did not quite know what was wrong with me.

"I heard my mom and dad discuss the trip outside my bedroom and it was obvious that mom would rather stay at home. Since they did not know what was wrong with me, they decided to take my little brother along with them. I was extremely upset, crying and carrying on, but nothing helped. Mom came in and hugged me goodbye. She smiled, but she looked very sad. 'Honey, be a good girl. Let Laura read you a story and rest as much as you can. I will be back before you wake up in the morning and we will have breakfast together.' Then she left quickly. Peter hollered 'so long' from the hallway, then I heard the car pull out of the driveway.

"That was the last time I saw my mother and brother. Somewhere during the night my father hit a telephone pole, the car was turned around and fell down an embankment. Apparently a passerby saw the skid marks and followed their tracks, finding my father, still inside the car, in a daze. My mother and little brother were thrown out of the vehicle. They were rushed to a hospital. My mother was dead, but my brother lived for two days before he died. My father had just a few scratches, and was kept for observation for a possible head injury. He came home three days later.

"All I remember is that nobody told me anything. My babysitter stayed overnight, and the next morning all our neighbors came with toys and gifts and no one would answer my questions. 'My mommy promised to have breakfast with me,' I kept saying and I refused to eat. When my doctor came later in the day, I became very agitated. I did not want to see him without mom in the room, but of all the cars that pulled up outside, none was our car. I could see the driveway from my bedroom window. The doctor gave me a shot, and all I remember is crying for my mom. Three days later, dad came home. He looked different. I knew that he had cried. It was only after the funeral that he told me that mom and Peter died in a car accident and he hoped I would be a big girl and help him. I was not willing to believe him. I spent days in bed daydreaming, talking to mom and asking her to come back home. I even promised to prepare breakfast for her, and to forget that she did not come back to keep her promise to me. I cleaned up my drawers and my whole bedroom, folded my shorts and blouses. We had always disagreed about keeping my room a bit neater. Now all my toys sat up on the shelf, the drawers looked neat. She would have to be pleased with me and come back home! I don't think I ate anything for several days. Lots of neighbors came and left.

"An aunt of mine came and stayed for several weeks, but I wanted nothing to do with her. I just wanted my mommy back home. Whenever I wanted to talk with dad about her, he became very angry. Once he yelled at me and asked me why I did not miss my brother. To tell you the truth, I don't think I ever thought about him. I wanted my mommy back, and all the rest of the world did not interest me until I found my mommy again."

In the meantime, her father mourned the death of his beloved son and rarely allowed himself to think of his wife. His guilt was so overwhelming, his grief so immense, that he was only able to cope "with one at a time" as he described it. Had father and daughter been able to mourn together for his wife — her mother — I am sure the result would have been less devastating, the denial less extreme. The loss could have been shared, and communication between father and daughter could have been reestablished. As it was, one year after the tragic double death, the father became more and more withdrawn and he finally sent his only surviving child to her grandparents. She had to start in a new school, thus losing the few girlfriends she had in her old school district. There she started to tell elaborate make-believe stories about her parents who temporarily had to move "far away," but had promised to return at the end of the school year when she would return to her old home.

She remained a loner, was often found to be extremely withdrawn, and still showed signs of great anxiety when cars pulled in or out of the driveway. She still had nightmares and, when she felt unobserved, would talk for very long times to an invisible person in a most animated fashion. When asked with whom she had such long conversations, she denied having talked to anyone.

I n my earlier book, *On Children and Death*, I told the story of a boy whose mother had died, and who was "caught" putting a big red apple on a window sill in the midst of winter in Chicago. When asked what this apple was doing there he bashfully stated, "Mommy always loved red apples. Maybe she will see it and come back home."

In our five-day live-in workshops which are held throughout the world, we try to help people get in touch with old, unfinished business. The loss of a parent is often the beginning of difficulties experienced later on in life. The inability to talk, share, and tell about the beloved and much missed parent sets the tone for future inability to share emotions and to learn — at an early age — to cope with loss and grief in a healthy fashion. If the surviving parent only knew how helpful it would have been for the child to show his sadness, to share tears together, later misery and negative patterns could be avoided.

Older children learn quickly when their behavior creates sadness or embarrassment for the rest of the family. They cry at night into the pillow, or go for long, lonely walks during which they often talk to the deceased parent. Trying to keep a lid on their emotions in the presence of other family members makes them awfully short tempered and vulnerable to outbursts of tears for the smallest reason. They get into fights with schoolmates and sometimes openly resent other children who are picked up from school, or for an outing, by their parents. They become defiant, daredevils in racing bicycles or go-carts, refusing to listen to adults who warn them to be more careful.

Pre-adolescents who lose a parent have a tendency to act out, become overly promiscuous, run away from home and get themselves into very dangerous life situations. Many of the adolescent prostitutes, who earn a marginal living by selling themselves, run away from home after the death of a parent. "I don't care a hoot" is the prevailing attitude, another form of denial. What they need the most is a pair of loving arms around them, a shoulder to lean on, and a grown-up who can give them permission to sob their hearts out. "I am not a baby anymore," is what they often say, but that is exactly what they are wishing to experience: to be babied, rocked, cradled, and loved until their hurt begins to heal.

It takes time to heal. It takes time to mourn. It doesn't matter how many weeks or months have passed. Everybody needs to be encouraged to take his time, to do it his own way. What work does for some, sleep will do for others. Party-going may be the answer for some teenagers, or adding a grotesque amount of make-up. Never judge or criticize anyone who tries to cope with the loss of a parent in his own way. There are coping mechanisms which may work for them that are inconceivable for you.

In families where there was a lot of fighting, physical punishment, and/or abuse, a lack of open and honest communications followed a sudden death. These families will have to work on a lot of unfinished business before healthy mourning can take place. Many men and woman who have been sexually abused in their childhood (a minimum of 30 percent of our population) finally get in touch with their long-suppressed rage, their sense of unfairness and their immense grief over the childhood they never had. Such "children in mourning" without a previous history of losses will have to learn first what it is that makes them almost chronically depressed, untrusting and withdrawn. Only after acknowledging the trauma (or multiple traumas of sexual abuse), can they be helped by expressing their hate, rage, aggression, and pain, their fear, grief and guilt on an inanimate object (our technique) i.e., shredding a telephone book to pieces, externalizing all their pent-up feelings they had kept locked inside for decades. Once this old unfinished business is expressed in a safe environment, in the presence of a supporting and unafraid helper, then will they begin the mourning process and cry for the death of a father. A father they may have loved as much as they feared or resented him.

If only we could help children in the early years and get them the help they need as soon as a trauma occurs, much unnecessary suffering could be avoided.

In contrast to sudden, unexpected deaths — which are usually much more difficult to deal with — death by cancer (or other slowly developing illnesses with a fatal outcome) give the surviving children a chance to make up for the past "misbehavior," to ask for forgiveness for months or years of silent treatment, or simply gives them an opportunity to solve old unfinished business with a dying parent. With so many young people now dying of AIDS, parents have an opportunity to do the same thing for their dying young adult children. Many a father who rejected his son for his homosexuality finally showed up during the last days of the son's life in order to avoid having to carry the guilt for the rest of his life. My most moving memory of such a moment was a father who literally hung around a hospital ward where his twenty-three-year-old son was dying. He refused to go in and face him, but he showed up every single day. One evening, shortly before the end of visiting hours, an orderly noticed him again. He stood behind the father and gently moved him to the door of his son's room. "Just come in with me and take a glimpse at him," he said ever so softly, opening the door at the same time. The father looked, and shocked at the appearance of the skeleton-like figure in the bed, abruptly stated: "This is not my son." A very small voice came from near the pillow, "Yes, dad, it's me, Richard, your son." The father hesitated, made a shy step towards his son, and minutes later their tears mingled as he leaned over his son, saying over and over again, "I'm sorry, I'm sorry . . ." I have never seen Richard with such a beaming expression on his face. "I knew you would come before it was too late," he said, "Now I can let go and die in peace . . ."

Another young mother I remember was from Minneapolis. She knew her days were numbered and although she had discussed her death and funeral with her husband, she never seemed to find the right words to explain to her children that she would not be around for the coming year. One night she pulled all her courage together and invited one after the other of her children to join her on the big king-size bed. With Susy, her nine-year-old, it was easy. They had always talked openly about a lot of things, and Susy knew inside that her mom was not getting well. The mother explained to her daughter that after her death she would always be in touch with her, and could hear her prayers and would be aware of her needs. Susy said, very matter-of-factly, "I know that you can read every thought of mine, hear every word I speak to you, although I cannot always hear your answer. That is not what bothers me. Do you think dad will bring another woman into our house who we would have to call mommy?" They laughed and cried together, and Susy was promised an evening discussion with dad to make sure (should such a thing ever occur) that Susy would not be forced to call "the other woman" mommy. Her son, Peter, had very different concerns. Who would cook dinner for them, and who would come to his games? A heart-to-heart talk helped the whole family to prepare for mom's eventual transition, and each one felt better for having had a chance to talk openly about this eventuality.

Adults facing the loss of their elderly parents would do well to discuss such an eventuality before a stroke or heart attack forces them to think about it. If they could sit and discuss the wishes of their parents with regard to treatment, hospitals they would prefer, funeral homes, estate and such in a calm, loving fashion with all the family members involved, it would go a long way to prepare them and save them a lot of worries and concerns. When all these decisions have been made ahead of time, in writing, when everybody present can be witness, not forced to think about such things in the midst of grief, shock and emotional turmoil can be lessened.

Death is but a transition from this life to another existence where there is no more pain and anguish. All the bitterness and disagreements will vanish, and the only thing that lives forever is LOVE. So love each other NOW, for we never know how long we will be blessed with the presence of those who gave us LIFE — no matter how imperfect many a parent has been.

"Everything can be bearable, when there was LOVE." This is perhaps the most important fact when we are dealing with the death of a parent. With the exception of tiny infants, every child will mourn the loss of a mother or father, even when they are grown and parents themselves.

The most significant variable of a relatively uncomplicated bereavement period or a prolonged and traumatic mourning depends to a great deal on the relationship the child and parent had, on the old unresolved conflicts that they carried within, on the level of communication they had. Last, but not least, is the mourner's earlier experiences with death and loss.

## Other books of interest from Celestial Arts:

**Don't Push the River**  by Barry Stevens

This classic work is a first-person account of the author's use of Gestalt Therapy and the ways of Zen, Krishnamurti, and the American Indian to see herself more clearly and lead a full and fulfilling life.

$12.95 paper, 280 pages

**The Essential Alan Watts**  by Alan Watts

Just before his death, Alan Watts completed this book, the project most dear to his heart. In it, he sets out the basic tenets of his philosophy, and provides guidelines for students and followers.

$8.95 paper, 180 pages

**Forget Me Not: Caring for and Coping with Your Aging Parents**  by Alan P. Siegal, M.D. and Robert Siegal

A handbook developed to help those caring for aging parents with dependent care needs including: immediate medical situations, emotional fallout, and help in finding resources needed for this important phase of life.

$9.95 paper, 156 pages

**Living in Hope: A 12-Step Approach**
by Cindy Mikluscak-Cooper, R.N. and Emmett E. Miller, M.D.

The first and only 12-step program for people who are HIV-positive, or at risk for infection. Using daily affirmations and guided imagery, this book provides powerful tools for coping, change, and healing.

$12.95 paper, 300 pages

**Love is Letting Go of Fear**  by Gerald Jampolsky, M.D.

The lessons in this extremely popular little book (over 1,000,000 in print), based on **A Course in Miracles**, will teach you to let go of fear and remember that our true essence is love. Includes daily exercises.

$7.95 paper or $9.95 cloth, 160 pages